FROM A
SIMPLE
MAN

FROM A
SIMPLE
MAN

RICHARD KRAMER

From a Simple Man

Copyright © 2023 by Richard Kramer. All rights reserved.

No part of this publication may be reproduced, stored in a retrieval system or transmitted in any way by any means, electronic, mechanical, photocopy, recording or otherwise without the prior permission of the author except as provided by USA copyright law.

The opinions expressed by the author are not necessarily those of URLink Print and Media.

1603 Capitol Ave., Suite 310 Cheyenne, Wyoming USA 82001
1-888-980-6523 | admin@urlinkpublishing.com

URLink Print and Media is committed to excellence in the publishing industry.

Book design copyright © 2023 by URLink Print and Media. All rights reserved.

Published in the United States of America

Library of Congress Control Number: 2023918455
ISBN 978-1-68486-533-8 (Paperback)
ISBN 978-1-68486-538-3 (Digital)

20.09.23

From a simple man, to a complex world.
From a heart of weakness.
To a world that is weaker.
From this time, to a time to come.

Acknowledgements

I first want to thank the Lord Jesus Christ, who has given me the inspiration and encouragement, with continual confirmation and peace, while writing His work. Through difficult times, tests and trials, the Lord has always been there for me.

I want to acknowledge Miriam Panek, who also has shown me encouragement to complete what I started. Who through faith and patience endured with me recent trials and tests in my life. Though at moments questioning her faith, held strong in spite of the effects my trials had on her. God bless her.

Contents

Acknowledgements 7
Introduction 11
Chapter 1   The Call—Armor of God........................15
Chapter 2   Freedom From Sin—The Face of Jesus...21
Chapter 3   Revelations—Speaking Out....................27
Chapter 4   Jerusalem—A Time Symbolic—
            Ministry to A Called Man 33
Chapter 5   The Most Holy Place—The Rod
            of Enablement 45
Chapter 6   Cloudy Times Ahead 49
Chapter 7   Foolish Prophets......................................57
Chapter 8   Final Thought and Prayer........................61
Chapter 9..65

Introduction

I have thought for many years, wondering if anything that I might say would be of value to anyone for any purpose.

I attempted to write, and make an account of my experiences as a Christian, years ago. I failed the Lord and did not finish the work, due to personal problems and setbacks in my personal life at that time. However, I know that the suffering in those days was later used by the Lord to help rid me of the hardness in my own heart and life. The struggles of that time caused me to learn to be at the total mercy of the Lord and to be in a frame of mind where I had to totally and completely rest in Him. David wrote, "It is good that I have been afflicted, that I may learn Thy statutes. The law of Thy mouth is better unto me than thousands of gold and silver." Psalm 119: 71-72. I now understand what he meant. I now have more peace. As time went on, and the years passed by, I began to be encouraged by the Lord to rewrite and make an account of my experiences. To write down the things that I have seen and heard and publish that which I have had understanding.

One day, this verse came clear and vivid in my mind while reconsidering. As I read it, I felt encouraged to continue. "The Lord gave the word: great was the company of those that published it." Psalms 68:11. Its purpose is for those who would read these things may believe. To have hope and a better understanding of certain truth and to develop a stronger faith in Him.

I have written this book, which is a testimony of my walk with the Lord and of the things that I have seen and heard, as well as what I have experienced in my life. All of which are experiences over my 57+ years as a Christian and believer in Yeshua (Jesus). I write to God's people and to the people of this nation. I testify of certain truth knowing that there are those who would disbelieve me or challenge what I say. I am able to deal with the fact that there are those who will not understand and maybe never will. I write to testify of the Lord God and things that He has shown me and taught me. My challenge is not to try and be convincing but to merely make an account of my experiences and how they occurred. My desire is to be obedient to the Lord and do as I have been encouraged to do. To bear witness to the truth as revealed to me. Though you will read things that seem unbelievable or presumptuous, I can only say that what I report about is, in fact, real and God is my witness. I can only assure you that I am as normal a person as anyone else; being an average person of average means, having the same joys and trials in this life as anyone else.

I am nothing special to anything, nothing special within myself. The one thing I do have, which is more desirable than wealth or stature, more precious than anything found in this world, is a strong relationship with Almighty God. I now possess the liberty and freedom not given in the world. I have more peace and clarity of mind that can only be given by the Lord. Without Him, there can only be turmoil and strife within, not to mention grief, dissatisfaction, and frustration. I have learned that, if you truly give *all* to Him as an exercise of faith, though it will indeed feel sacrificial, in time you will begin to see that your needs are truly more than fulfilled, possessing all through Him in the spirit of love and comfort. This creates, within us, the growing sense of rest that we are all called to.

I have truly experienced life, at times, as a place in the desert. A place of testing and trial, a place of refining and finishing, a place of thirst, hunger, and toil, where the winds and sands of adversity always blow. I will, however, testify that as a son of the Living God, he has proven to always be there with me, providing the filling of my soul and spirit to keep me going. The personal trials of this life are, indeed, nothing to be compared to what lies ahead when entering into His rest. They especially cannot be compared to the hereafter.

I have caught a glimpse of such things, as I have recorded in this book, and I know that to all who believe in the Lord Jesus Christ, the God of Abraham, Issac, and Jacob, comes a hereafter that is more wonderful that words can describe. A time held only by the Lord, in a kingdom of laws and justice, not understood by many. "Of the increase of His government and peace, there shall be no end. Upon the throne of David, and upon His kingdom. To order it, and to establish it with justice and righteousness from henceforth even forever." Isaiah 9:7.

Chapter One

The Call—Armor of God

It was many years ago, when I decided that I needed to have the Lord in my life. I remember, as a child, having an instilled belief, knowing down deep that the Lord was somehow with me. As most children, I did not ascribe to much that was religious. However, when in need, I found myself crying out to God for help. I somehow knew, down deep, that He heard me and there was always something inside me, drawing me. In later years, as an adult, the yearning grew and I found myself going forward in a church altar call to publicly receive Jesus as my Savior.

It was in the summertime, in a small town church in southern Minnesota, during an Evangelist's meeting, that I publicly professed my belief in Jesus as my Lord and Savior. It was then that I began to see changes in my life. The changes begin spiritually. I was having stronger feelings of being pulled toward something. At the same time, I was having sensations of great peace in my heart, deep within my being. I knew that it was the presence of the Lord. Also, in those days, there was an ever-growing yearning, an almost painful desire, to know more and more of the peace that I was feeling. My inner longing was to have as close a relationship as I could, wanting to know more of the Lord's presence, and to, perhaps, hear His voice.

I soon began a time of great spiritual growth, a phase of training perhaps. It came like an exposure, or an awareness of knowledge, about selected people and various circumstances in their lives. I had a sensitivity and clear knowledge of what troubled people. I knew the absolute truth of what was causing them trouble. Whether it be rebellion or sin, selfishness or vanity, or spiritual warfare; all of which was revelation from the Lord and only revelation from Him, all of which was without failure of being true and accurate, all of which became clearer and clearer to me as time went on and as the Lord allowed. The truth of the revelations always prevailed, never once being wrong. Proven by those whose testimonies admitted that what I said to them was right in my attempts to minister and discuss their various needs, bringing to surface underlying issues that lead to repentance.

These assigned or, perhaps, divine appointments continued off and on for about a year or so. Then one day, while sitting at my desk at home, something very wonderful happened. A scripture verse became more than vivid and clear in my mind. Out of curiosity, I grabbed my Bible, which was on my desk, and I looked up the verse and began to read these words: "Put on the whole armor God, that you may be able to stand against the wiles of the Devil. For we wrestle not against flesh and blood, but against principalities, against powers, against the rulers of the darkness of this world, against spiritual wickedness in high places. Wherefore, take unto you the whole armor of God, that you may be able to withstand in the evil day, and having done all to stand, stand therefore, having your loins girt about with truth, and having the breastplate of righteousness, and above all, taking the shield of faith, with which you shall be able to quench all the fiery darts of the wicked, and take the helmet of salvation, and the sword of the spirit, which is the word of God; praying with all prayer and supplication in the spirit, and watching thereunto with all perseverance and supplication for all Saints." Ephesians 6:11-18.

As I began to read the scripture, the presence of the Lord came upon me with light, which seemed to fill the room with peace. I could hear what I thought was the quiet voice of the Lord, as if He was speaking the words right to my heart. I began to weep and tremble, and the more I read, the more I wept and trembled. I was crying to the point where I could not see, having to wipe my eyes to be able to read. When I finished reading, the trembling eased, and I continued to cry and cry with overwhelming peace in my heart that welled up within me. With this, I felt exhilarated, excited, and expectant, knowing that somehow all will be okay. The trembling soon stopped, and the room was quiet. What remained was the most amazing sense of joy, with the feelings of comfort and awareness that I had never felt before.

For days and days I tried to function with these overwhelming feelings. As I would think back on the experience, I could not help but break out in tears of joy, praising the Lord in my heart, knowing fully that I was visited by the Lord Himself and actually heard His voice. From that point on, I somehow knew that I would not need to do anything in my own strength and that I could rely on God in all that I did. I also somehow knew that I was being prepared for something, not to mention the new beginnings of a way of life, and a very close walk with Him. I now understand that the wearing of the "armor of God" requires a life of faith. It is the protection of the mind, body, and heart that is important for a Christian to grow. It is necessary to put one's absolute trust in Christ and to be completely dependant on Him in everything. Even when darkness seems to prevail in this life, we must know that all that is evil remains subservient to the will of God. As the scripture says, "that for by Him all things were created, that are in Heaven, and that are in the Earth, visible and invisible, whether there be thrones or dominions, or principalities, or powers, all things were created by Him, and for Him." Col. 1:16.

As the scripture also says, "I am the Lord and there is none else. I form the light and create darkness, I make peace and create evil, I, the Lord, do all these things." Isaiah 45:6-7.

Chapter Two

Freedom From Sin—
The Face of Jesus

Here is a verse that, again, came more than vivid in my mind and heart and though I had no experience as I had before, it sort of stayed with me: "I will bless the Lord, who has given me counsel: my heart also instructs me in the night seasons." Psalms 16:7.

Some months had passed and I was still feeling very expectant of what was to come, not knowing exactly what, however, I was excited and willing to accept anything. I was growing in faith and in the knowledge of the Lord and trying to live normally, as one attempts to do in this world. I was also ministering to people's needs as the Lord allowed and revealed. I could do nothing to help anyone unless the Lord opened a way. Unexpectedly, one evening while sleeping, I was taken up, as it were, in a dream and saw a vision. I was fully aware and totally alert when, suddenly, I somehow knew that I arrived where I was to be taken. I was suddenly drawn towards something and began walking. I became aware that it was quite dark, though I assumed it was because it was the middle of the night. I came upon what appeared to be an encampment resembling a prison, a dark and sad place. I approached what was like a very high, wire-linked type fence. Inside the encampment the lighting was very dim, sort of grayish, much like that of the early evening on a dark, cloudy day. I looked more closely through the fence as I walked right up to it, and I would see stonewalls and buildings beyond, also grayish in color. I could see that it was a very large place, isolated and alone, all to itself. While standing there looking through the fence, I could see what appeared to be people, lost souls, walking about sort of aimlessly with nowhere to go, imprisoned by sin.

A moment later, some women had become aware of me standing there outside the fence and came over to me. I could not hear sounds or voices as a couple of the women attempted to speak to me and draw my attention to them and lure me in. I suddenly felt something pulling at my will and mind. I became aware that all that was inside the encampment was evil and sensual, and its lure and strength over me was more than I could bear. I felt like I was being drawn into its grip. At the point of being overwhelmed and taken in, I was then suddenly drawn back away. The luring and what was tempting me had stopped.

I stood for a moment and turned around. What I then saw was what appeared to be a man standing off in the far distance. He was standing as if he were overseeing the event that had just happened to me, watching out for my safety I was somehow rapidly taken over to the man, and I stood looking at him for a moment. I was drawn closer, close enough to be able to reach out and touch him. I was then shown his face, which shined with a soft glow of light. I could see his countenance, which seemed to be that of an average man. I then saw two facial expressions; one was that of great overwhelming wisdom, the other was that of great overwhelming strength.

I was looking very attentively at his face and could see what was scarring on his left jaw and cheek, where there was once hair from a beard. I then looked at his eyes, which at first seemed like any other person's eyes. As I looked closer, he then closed his eyes and opened them. I was yet drawn closer to see his eyes more clearly, and they began to glow with intenseness.

At that moment, I was given to understand that this man was my Savior, Jesus. He then reached out and grabbed a hold of me, grabbing me by my upper arms near my shoulders. I could feel His great hands as

He squeezed and lifted me up. As He raised me, I was drawn even closer to His face and to Himself. His eyes grew brighter as I was raised up and drawn through His eyes into Himself. In Him, I could see all that is eternal and forever. I was shown eternity as the sky, as far as it was all around me. I could see that there was no end; there was no end. He gave me a moment to look and see, and I beheld.

The very next thing I knew was that I was being lowered back down, back onto my bed. I was wide awake, having a clear and complete memory of what just took place. I was having the same feelings of inner peace as I have had before, knowing in my heart, and without question, that this was the presence of the Lord; I was delivered from the grip of sin, with its overwhelming power that seemed to overcome me. I was placed into the Lord Himself, as I looked upon His face and beheld His eyes that burned, indeed, like the amber flame of a fire. For days and days later, I had great contentment knowing that I was in the Lord and He was in me, and together we now live.

I have seen His wisdom. It is wisdom of the ages, wisdom of all that is eternal, and it knows the depths of life and creation. I know now that I can fully rely on His wisdom, and that it is foolish and vain to attempt to rely on anything of my own. I have seen His strength.

It is strength and power held by no other. Strength and power so strong that it controls the very intricacy of life and creation and all its aspects.

Who am I to be so chosen to have this happen, that only those of scripture have experienced? I think of Moses in Genesis 33:11, I think of Jacob in Genesis 32:30, I think of David in Psalms 27:8, I think of Daniel in Daniel 10:10-12, and I also think of John in Revelation 20:11.

I have, indeed, seen the face of Him who is the Eternal One. Whatever the purpose the Lord had in doing this for me, I did not know at that time.

Chapter Three

Revelations—Speaking Out

During the months following, I had continual questions as to the meaning of this experience, though I had no answers. I was, however, getting a tremendous amount of encouragement from the Lord. What was coming in my life was unknown, and I did not care. Some time had passed, and I was having more exposure by the Lord in spiritual matters. I, by revelation from the Lord, could discern the presence of darkness and that which was evil. I began to be able to discern what it was and identify how it affected those people in whom the Lord revealed to me. By revelation, I could identify the sins in the heart of a person. I could identify the true and real motives, in spite of any false reasoning people gave or knowing anything of the prevailing facts. I could do nothing with the revelations and the understanding that I had to help anyone, unless the Lord opened the way. I was also, however, to try and learn and have understanding. I know now that there are many, many people functioning in life with various depths of falsehood and misunderstandings governing their thoughts and actions of their lives. People are yielding to lower levels, causing mistakes and sin, all of which are overshadowed by lacking knowledge of the inner most part of their own heart and all of which are overshadowed by the lack of being aware of the schemes of evil, and setting up a standard being one's total trust in the word of God.

At one point, while the Lord was exposing me in spiritual matters, I became so sensitive and attuned to the things He was revealing, that once during a prayer meeting in a church that I was just starting to attend, I spoke out.

It was a Wednesday night meeting consisting of about thirty people, including the pastor and his wife. We were sitting in a partial circle facing those playing the music. The meeting seemed to be going along normally. The pastor was leading the group and the music. He also gave a small talk on love. There was music, prayers, and sharing of needs, and people seemed to be enjoying themselves. However, all during the service I was getting strong urges from the Lord, and I felt that there was clearly something wrong. It was building within me as the meeting progressed. I felt surges of strength within me, which seemed that it needed to be released by speaking. The meeting was drawing to an end, and they had just finished a song, so the Pastor asked if anyone else had anything to add. By then I was completely overpowered by the Lord within me, and I just, at that moment, bolted to my feet. Without my control, my left hand was in the air and my right hand was pointing, and I began to speak what would be very hard words. The words flowed out as if I was venting the Lord's frustration. As I stood, my eyes were closed, and I began to move to my right around the inside of the circle of people. I was pointing and calling out publicly the inner thoughts and sins prevailing in each of the person's lives that I had stopped in front of and confronted. I spoke out only as it was revealed to me. To one I spoke of sexual immorality, to another hardness of heart, to another lying and deceiving. Around the circle I went, This went on for several minutes, as I addressed about ten people.

When the experience was over, I was standing between the circle of people and those playing the music. The room was in total silence. I then began to hear sobbing and weeping from various locations within the group. Moments had gone by, and a woman spoke up and confessed openly that what I said about her was true; she repented publicly to the group. Then someone else stood and confessed, then another, and yet another. Each and all of those that I stopped in front of and spoke out against unanimously confessed that what I had revealed to the group was true, except for one who will go unnamed. Suddenly, a Scripture was then read by one of the musicians, and then another Scripture was read by someone else.

One very serious thing that came out as a result of the event was that the pastor's son had sexually molested a couple of the younger girls in the church at various church gatherings. A fact that I was certainly not aware of prior to that night.

The meeting was over and music resumed with one more song. I personally felt a sense of being vulnerable and exposed, until people approached me to thank me. A woman from the back of the group came up to me and told me that I had done well with the Lord, and that he sometimes has us do things we may not understand. With this, I left the church. For several days following, I had the same peace and feelings of the presence of the Lord with me.

The pastor was in complete disadvantage of the experience and was in denial. Days later, he requested of each member, privately, that those who believed me should leave the church and follow me, thinking perhaps that I might start a new church. It was never my intention to have the church split up like that and, most certainly, never my intention to start a church. The people who did leave the church left out of their own convictions.

The message given was to expose the truth. The truth was revealed, confirmed by those who openly admitted that what I said about them was true. The church and the names of those involved shall go unnamed. I see no reason to reveal, to anyone, the darkness which overcame a group of people. There was no reason at this point to expose and embarrass anyone for their faults. After all, "all have sinned, and have fallen short of the glory." Romans 3:23.

Chapter Four

Jerusalem—A Time Symbolic— Ministry to A Called Man

Some time had passed, perhaps a year or so. I was attending another church, different from where anyone else I had known at that time was going. I was beginning to catch sight of the fact that the Lord was showing me that He had different things for me to experience; things other than the dark and perhaps demonic side. It had now become time for me to focus on something new.

One Sunday in the springtime on a warm, beautiful day, I went to church. I was not expecting much, I was just thankful winter was over. During the service, as the pastor was speaking, the presence of the Lord came to me as a jolt of peace and trembling in my heart, saying, "go unto Jerusalem and abide there." It came to me unexpectedly, and I began to have feelings of excitement, knowing that I was about to hear from the Lord again. Moments later, it came to me again, saying "go unto Jerusalem and abide there." It came to me hard and, sitting among a packed church, I began to weep and tremble. I felt as though I had no strength, as if I could have slid off the pew onto the floor in full view of those sitting around me. Again it came to me, moments later, saying in my heart, "go unto Jerusalem and abide there." By this time, I was outright crying and trembling. I actually had to support myself from falling. I am sure it must have been strange for those sitting around me, seeing me carry on that way as I did, but I knew, without question, I must go.

It was the very next day that I began to make arrangements to go to Israel. It took a few weeks to get ready, in that I needed to obtain a passport and make plans necessary for me to be gone. During the time it took me to make the arrangements, I received confirmation and encouragement from the Lord about going. In addition, I realized I was about to have a personal tour of Jerusalem, and that there would be an agenda to follow with a purpose. This would be mostly prayer time with the Lord, and the purpose of the trip would be revealed once I got there.

I had finally arrived in Tel Aviv and took a bus to Jerusalem. I stayed in a hotel not far from the west side of the old city. I believe it is now called the Jerusalem Plaza. From the 11th floor of my hotel room, I had a clear view of the Jaffa Gate. That first morning, I was anxious to go into the old city. As I opened the door to leave from my room, there was a bouquet of flowers and a card sitting outside my door. The card read, "To a very special guest." I was not sure if the flowers and card were a mistake or not. No one really knew where I was staying. I looked down the hallway in both directions, and mine was the only room with flowers at the door. I assumed it was because I was a new check-in.

I left the hotel and took a taxi to the Damascus Gate. I stopped in front of the gate and looked at it in amazement, realizing within myself that I was truly there. I spoke out these words: "Jerusalem, Jerusalem, the faithful city."

I entered through the gate and walked through the old city. I took my time and kind of wandered about, taking in the sights. I was sort of pondering what I was to find. I visited the Wailing Wall and walked my way back north, through the old city, back to the Damascus Gate. I stopped, only briefly, to purchase a duffel bag that I needed from a small shop.

Just outside the Damascus Gate, there was street I walked down and came upon a place called the Garden Tomb, the place outside the old city walls where Jesus was believed to be buried. I entered the Garden Tomb through a bookstore that was there. I noticed that there was a park area outside the bookstore that had areas arranged for church groups to have services at the site of the Lord's burial. I walked about the Garden Park area and came upon a railing where you could look upon a hillside called Golgotha. I stood for several minutes. Suddenly, I noticed a young, Arab man was standing next to me, looking straight at me and crying. As I turned to address him, he spoke to me in broken English, introducing himself as Basim. He then asked me if I knew the one they call Jesus. I said that I did and asked him why he was crying. He explained to me that he had been searching for Him, and wanted to know all that I knew of Him. We sat at a nearby bench and after answering his many questions, Basim prayed to receive Jesus into his life. Basim soon stopped crying, and I could see joy on his face as he began to smile. He then thanked me.

I had not realized it then, but I had just witnessed a man being saved at the tomb of Christ. I later thought it an honor to have part in it, there in Jerusalem. Basim asked me how I was planning to get around and where all that I wanted to go. He was so grateful that he offered to chauffer me to anywhere in Israel. He even offered some suggestions. I explained that my intentions were to stay in the Jerusalem area. He then insisted that he take me to wherever I was going each day of my stay.

He only asked that he would have some time free to sell olivewood carvings at the tourist stops, which he sold from the trunk of his car.

I spent the rest of the day with Basim. In the evening he drove me back to the hotel. Once he dropped me off, he was heading home to his family to tell them what had happened to him that day. Before leaving me, he announced he would be by the next morning about 9:00am. That night I realized that the Lord had just made arrangements for me to not only pray with Basim, but he allowed for my transportation during my stay. That evening, I wondered what would be the plan for the next day.

I was able to open wide the window of my room and look out. While looking out over the old city and enjoying the lights, I had observed how the city had looked at night. I also took in the evening sky. Looking south, I wondered if, perhaps, we could go to Bethlehem.

The next morning came. As I was leaving my room, I opened the door and there sat another bunch of flowers and a basket of fruit. I, of course, brought them in and left. I went out the front of the hotel and, sure enough, there was Basim already pulled up and waiting. He greeted me with his broken English and said, "Good morning, brother." As I got into the car, his next words were, "Perhaps we go to Bethlehem today, okay? I take you." I took that as a directive from the Lord, being that I was just previously wondering that myself during the night. So we went.

We spent most of the day in Bethlehem, seeing what Basim thought I should see, including the place where he bought his olivewood carvings. We spent all of the afternoon at Shepard's Field, talking about Jesus and what life was like in the United. States. It was all I could do to answer his many questions. Later that evening, we returned to Jerusalem and he took me back to the hotel.

The next morning, I found a basket of fruit and a vase with a couple of flowers. I placed them with the others I had received and while leaving the room, I noticed that my room was again the only room to have anything at the door. I proceeded to the front of the hotel, and there again was Basim, promptly at 9:00am. His plan was to take me to the Dung Gate and drop me off there. He wanted to be there when the tour buses arrived, so that he could try and sell the olivewood carvings because he sold nothing the day before, spending the whole day with me. I of course agreed. We made plans to meet up again later at the Garden Tomb. As Basim was parking his car, I walked across the street through the Dung Gate, down the walkway to the Wailing Wall area.

I could not help being attracted to a couple of young groups of school children. The spirit within me jumped for joy as each group began singing. As I passed by them, I noticed they were singing songs of praise.

I spent a lot of time observing the Wailing Wall area and its bustle. I had made my way up to the dome of the rock and remembered that this was the original site of the Temple. No longer there, I was thinking how nice it would be to see. In the afternoon, I proceeded north through the old city, back through the Damascus Gate, and arrived at the Garden tomb. As I entered the park area, I noticed a church group having a service at one of the areas provided. I sat down in back of the group, about eight or ten rows from anyone. My intention was to spend some quiet time there and read my Bible that I carried with me. The group then proceeded to serve Communion, just as I was sitting. I never expected to have Communion until a nice lady, who was standing on my left side of the group helping pass the trays, gestured to a man on my right side, indicating that they should serve me. They came all the way back and served me. I saw that as the Lord's arrangement for me to have Communion that day.

Later in the afternoon, Basim arrived. We spent a little time there at the Garden Tomb, and then Basim drove me back to the hotel. That evening, Basim returned to the hotel, knocking at my door. He wanted me to meet some of his friends, so we went out to a small café just inside the Jaffa Gate. I met his friends and we had tea.

The next morning, I again received flowers and fruit. Basim, again, was prompt a 9:00am. We drove around the old city to the Mount of Olives. We spent a lot of time there talking about Jesus and, of course, he had his never-ending questions.

There was a real purpose for me to be spending so much time with Basim, talking about Jesus. I felt that here was a young Arab man who needed to hear certain things from me and have as many questions answered as he could before I left Jerusalem.

We later drove to the Lion's Gate, and Basim showed me the upper room so I could see where the Last Supper had taken place. The upper room is upstairs over the King David shrine. Basim then again drove me back to the hotel. That evening, while praying in my room, a verse of Scripture came vivid in my heart. I looked up the Scripture and read these words: "To him that overcometh, will I give to eat of the tree of life, which is in the midst of the paradise of God." Revelation 2:7B. I was unsure of what the Lord was saying to me until I arrived the next day at the Garden Tomb.

I spent a couple of hours while waiting for Basim praying and walking about. I was thinking of that verse. Thinking to myself, over and over, *tree of life, tree of life*. I, at that moment, came upon a small lemon tree. I noticed that there was literally only one lemon on it. Out of curiosity, I combed through the entire Garden Tomb area to see if there was any other fruit tree. There were a lot of trees but only one had fruit on it, that small lemon tree. That one lemon was, indeed, the only fruit in the entire area. There was no question, that fruit was there for me.

I stepped over some landscaping to reach the fruit, and I grabbed it. I began eating the lemon. The thing that I first realized, of course, was that the lemon was bitter. While eating, I had thought that the bitterness was not only real, but symbolic as well, just as the other events of each day were. That final evening, Basim drove me around various parts of Jerusalem to show me things that he thought I should see.

My trip to Jerusalem started where I had prayed with someone to receive Christ, and he not only became my friend, but provided my transportation throughout the city. I had visited Bethlehem, the city where the Lord's life on this earth began. I was able to walk through the old city, seeing the temple area and the Wailing Wall. I was in the upper room where the Lord had his last Passover feast with his disciples. I had Communion in the Garden Tomb where Christ was buried and rose again. I walked on the Mount of Olives, where Jesus bled as he wept before His death. I saw Golgotha, above where He was hung on the cross to die. I also saw the tomb where He was laid to rest. Finally, I tasted of the bitterness of His last days on Earth.

The purpose of my trip was now fulfilled. I am blessed of God to have been there. The one thing, however, that I could not see was the actual Temple itself. My time in Jerusalem was over. I had seven days of prayer and quietness; a time of reflection and being with the Lord, a time symbolic in the city of my God, a tour that had spiritual meaning for me, a purpose. Part of that purpose had to do with Basim, a new Christian that the Lord saw fit for me to be a part of his first beginnings in his walk with God.

My last day was drawing to a close. That afternoon, I was sitting in a park west of the old city reading, when a small Jewish boy walked up to me and spat on me. As he walked by, I felt this was definitely something symbolic. I was not sure how to take that, or what may have been meant by that, but I did feel, somehow, a certain rejection. I just stood up and watched as the boy ran off.

Basim stopped by the hotel that evening to say goodbye. He thanked me for the time we spent together. He felt the Lord had something special for him as well. I assured him that there was. He was thankful for being saved and for the time we shared. I gave to Basim the remaining fruit and flowers that were left over from my stay, as well as money for his time and gasoline. He was crying when he left the room, knowing that the Lord brought us together, and we had become friends and brothers in the Lord. Basim felt sorrow that we may never see each other again until the last day, at the sound of Shofar, when the trumpet is blown and we are caught up to be in the presence of the Lord.

As far as the flowers and the fruit, I am not sure. I only know that my room was the only room to receive them. One thing for sure, I did feel like a very special guest.

Chapter Five

The Most Holy Place—
The Rod of Enablement

"Thou hast set my feet in a large room." Psalms 31:8.

Life was proceeding after my return from Jerusalem. I had been pondering what it might be like to serve the Lord in a full-time capacity. I was not sure what or how, or if it made any difference to the way that I had already been serving. I just only knew that I was having yearnings and wanted to be closer to God. As time went by, I began to question somehow what was to come and what would lie ahead.

Then one night, again while sleeping, I was caught up in the spirit and seeing a dream. I was taken to a brightly lit city. I began walking along a narrow street and noticed that all the walls and houses were much like what I had seen in Jerusalem. It was light without the sun, almost golden in color. I was given to understand that this was the city of the Lord. The city was very old and ancient, as old as any city ever was, yet, it also had the feeling of being very new.

I began walking along another street, facing east. The street suddenly ramped downward to the right as I passed under an archway, narrowing between two walls. I continued east to a crossing street and turned right, facing south. I walked south to an open entryway on my right. I turned to the right, entering another archway. I went up the large steps to a very large, double doorway and went in. Upon entering through the large doorway, I came into a large room. I crossed over the raised floor about halfway and stopped. I was standing in the center of a vast room. As I turned to my left, I could see that the floor was a deep blue color, with white curving and floral designs. As I attempted to observe the floor, my attention was drawn to the appearance of the most amazing, sparkling, bright light that suddenly emerged. The brightness filled the room and overcame the vast space. I looked into the brightness of the light and from an elevated position, the Lord's right hand appeared and in it was His staff. His hand and staff rose as I thought the Lord stood. It came toward me, as if to touch me. As He rose, I had fallen backwards to the floor on my right side. As I fell, there was a glimpse of a great throne behind the Lord, and the brightness overcame me. The brightness was so intense, I could see no details of the floor, or the throne, or His staff.

I braced myself up on my right elbow, still being on the floor, continuing to look up. I had my left arm raised, as if to shield my eyes from the light. Peace absolutely overwhelmed me. I knew that I was in the most Holy place. I was in the very presence of God Himself.

The Lord raised me to my feet, and I bowed before Him. I was given a moment to see the Lord's right hand and staff, which was blurred by the brightness of the light. I was then let out to my left and walked back out through the large doorway. While approaching the archway and going through it, I was then suddenly back on my bed, fully aware and awake.

I am blessed by the Lord to have been taken to the Holy city and brought to the most Holy place. I am not only blessed, I am thankful to have been able to behold His presence.

I was returned to Jerusalem to see the Temple, which I could not see during my trip. I am thankful to have gone back, as it were, to the Temple to see it as it really is. I love the Lord with all my heart, with all my strength, and with all my being. I am nothing within myself, nothing without Him. I am in the Lord, and He is within me. Together we live.

May I always please the Lord, for I am struck with love that He chose me for His purpose. May I always fulfill His purpose and bring Him joy. May I always be with Him, to know His innermost heart and the depth of Himself.

Day and night, my spirit longs for Him. Day and night, He is with me, guiding and protecting me.

Show me your ways, o Lord, that I may show others, so that they may see and believe, and come to the truth of You.

Chapter Six

Cloudy Times Ahead

"Now, therefore, speak to the men of Judah, and to the inhabitants of Jerusalem, saying thus sayeth the Lord, behold, I frame evil against you, and devise a plan against you; return, now, everyone from his evil ways, and make your ways good." Jeremiah 18:11

One evening this verse came, again vivid and clear, to me at a low point in my life. At that time, I was not sure why, yet I continued to be encouraged of the Lord about many things, while suffering through some very personal hardships and setbacks. I also continued to have those times of knowing His presence and feeling peace in my heart. I had taken an interest, in those days, over the issues of prophecy. Like many people, I was attempting to understand what I could and observe how the issues of prophecy were particular for today.

Prophecy was an area that the Lord first began to use on me to get my attention, even prior to my salvation. I have always had a keen interest in the troubles of our world. Being observant of the severity of change and how changes affect life, I now know full well the Lord is in the center of it all and continues to be. In spite of the many questions we all may have, particularly the questions we have on human suffering. I was developing concerns about our country over the years of my life. I have seen, like everyone else, internal change that was concerning me. There has been change in people's focus, on what is really important to them; change in morals and in attitudes about life, and an apparent falling away from the Lord in the fabric of the heart of our country. Of the changes this country could go through, falling away from the Lord is the most critical. If we, as a people, are to continue in the blessing we enjoy, we must always look to Him.

Over time, my concerns about this country were growing. I am fearful of what could become of our morals, our politics, our economy, and the future of our children.

Much time again had passed, and then, again, one evening while sleeping, I was taken up in the spirit, awakened from my sleep. I was lifted up into the evening sky. There were two angels, one on each side of me.

They had grabbed me by my wrists and up under each arm, being behind me. We rose up fast into the night sky. I could see the stars as they took me northward, then turning west. I could feel their grip on my arms and wrists as we went out over our country, out over the Pacific Ocean, a great distance. I could see the moonlight shining off the water as the angels then turned me around, looking back over this country. I then could see the landmass. The sun was just barely beginning to emerge over the horizon. I could see how the very early morning light had shone on the ground. I was made to look down, to focus on our country, and to see our nation as it really is. As I looked for a moment, there suddenly appeared the most frightful thing: a huge cloud completely covering the land. The thickness was from the surface of the Earth to as high up as I was.

The top of the cloud mass was bright and light, being lit by the emerging sun. The bottom of the cloud mass was darkened and black, having the appearance of the severest of storms. There was strong wind, lightning and thunder everywhere. There was no place to hide or escape; a frightful sight of dismay and turmoil. I was given a moment to look, knowing that this storm not only was from the Lord but was doing its job.

The cloud was then suddenly gone, and the angels began to take me back. I remember hearing the sound of their wings as we proceeded back. We returned more directly and more swiftly to bring me home. As we approached my house, I was then suddenly back on my bed, fully awake and fully aware of what just happened. Being concerned about what I had just seen, I went to the Lord and asked what the meaning of this vision was. I questioned: Was judgment coming to this nation? I received no answer at that time.

Days later, while praying and reading the Scripture, these words I felt in my heart: "The knowledge of the Lord is not found in the children." I caught a clear sight in my heart that there are now generations of children in this country growing up without ever hearing of the Lord and of His gospel and what it means. There was confirmation to that one day in a park I had stopped at to read, as two boys about twelve years in age approached me and sat by me. One of them had asked me what I was reading. I told them that I was reading the Bible. They had never heard of it and did not know what it was about. This truth reaffirmed to me that there are children in this country who will soon become adults, entering into every facet and fiber in this society, bringing forth a nation not grounded in the faith that founded it. Our nation's children are becoming adults and not grounded in the convictions of what blesses a nation. If these new generations of people that are not grounded in the convictions of God, how much more distant from God and the truth of His blessings that we have, develop? Our nation, founded on scriptural principles, is now at a crossroad. I must address all people, and we must ask ourselves the question: What will happen to this country should the Lord's blessing change? Have we, as a civilization, already gone through our beginnings and growth? Have we reached our peak as a society? Are we now seeing the beginnings of our decline, as all nations and civilizations of the past have experienced? I believe we have lost our inner strength. A nation of power and stature, blessed by the Lord from its beginning, is now looking into the face of change. Another confirmation of the Lord's displeasure came to me while writing this very chapter.

While returning home one evening, during a rainstorm and threats of a tornado and strong wind, I passed by an American flag lying soaking wet in the street, right at the intersection where I turn in to my home. Somehow, the wind had blown that flag, with its piece of broken mounting, almost to my front door. I watched that flag while waiting to turn. I first wondered how long it had been there. I could not help but see people driving their cars over the flag, trampling over it, so to speak. No one having respect enough to stop and pick it up, not even two police cars parked in the complex front parking lot that had to pass by the flag to enter the complex. I now have that flag. A sign from the Lord to keep writing, to be encouraged that what I know is really true.

The very symbol of honor and stature and power in this world lying wet and tattered, ignored by its own people, as well as those who are to enforce its laws and rights. That flag was blown down in the storm. What will blow down in the storm that I saw? We need repentance, with change of attitudes, as well as our people returning to the ways of our fathers, or our country faces the possibility of falling from within itself; where its abundance continues to find itself going overseas.

If the people do not hear and listen, and if the people do not yield to the warnings given, this country will be terrorized by its own defeat. By no means is my warning new. By no means can people say that they have not heard. I fear for our families, where more than half now are being broken apart by divorce. I fear for the economics which are challenged by global change, as much of our product, once made here, is now being made overseas. I fear for our politics, which has the appearance of overthrow; the left fighting the right. I fear for our laws, where the balances of justice seem to be tipping. I fear for our morals, where sexually driven attitudes burn like fire.

The will of this nation must change. The heart of this nation must return to the ways of the Lord. The knowledge of the Lord must be given to all. If the children do not know God, who will teach of Him in the years to come? Who will spread the good news of salvation amongst the growing hardship and suffering? Who will speak peace to the people in the midst of prevailing evil?

As strong as our country seems, it's heart is weakened. We know of unity, and united we stand. The kind of unity we need to face coming change will never be achieved, unless the Lord Himself is in the middle of its design. Do we, as a people, really put our trust in Him? Are our leaders truly attempting to put the needs of this nation in His hands? With all of the evidence of so many political differences and agenda extremes, I really wonder.

The call to repentance and change is given. The word to "The men of Judah, and the inhabitants of Jerusalem" has been told. Now, will the heart of the nation return? Will this nation continue to grow and prosper? Will this country no longer see attacks from its enemies? Will the division of politics heal? Will the balances of justice be restored? Will all the sexual immoralities continue? My answer to these questions is: Will we, as a people, repent and change?

Chapter Seven

Foolish Prophets

One evening, while I was just beginning to relax from the day and thinking of the things that I have been writing, another verse was impressed upon me and became clear and vivid in my heart. I got my Bible and read. "And the word of the Lord came to me, saying, son of man, prophesy against the prophets of Israel that prophesy, and say thou unto them that prophesy out of their own hearts, hear ye the word of the Lord. Thus sayeth the Lord God: whoa unto the foolish prophets, that follow their own spirit, and have seen nothing. O Israel, thy prophets are like foxes in the desert." Ezekiel 13: 2-3.

Concerning the teaching of our people and the children, I address the issue of all those doing the various religious teaching. The Lord is against you, you who teach falsely the word of God. You, through your own ideas and understanding, and by your own spirit, lead people amiss. This country is riddled with false teaching and doctrine. Many of God's people are being seduced by teachers and leaders of Christianity, who by their own vanity and lies attempt to build their own walls and monuments, using the words of peace to gain profit and acclaim.

The Lord's right hand is against those people and those organizations, who through divining and divination mislead people. There can no longer be teaching that presumes God's word and His will, calling it faith, to manipulate God's word for gain. Those who lead are held in strict accountability. Credibility and honesty are a must to serve God. How can those who distort God's truth, who say that He has spoken when He has not, be found in the assembly of God's people? How can they be found in the writings of the House of Israel, when false hope has been taught to the children and to those seeking the truth of Him? Through the fierceness of the Lord's anger, there will now be strong wind, rain, and hailstorms to break down the walls of these particular voices. The truth of these ministries will be revealed, and the Lord's hand will be against them.

Haven't we seen enough of the ministries in the past exposed? Haven't we seen enough sin in the lives of leadership and religious organizations? Sadness develops in the heart of people and serious questions of life arise when people find out that there has been misleading issues, and when secrets revealed about leaders lie contrary to the word of God and the calling of leadership. Teaching God's word is not the business of strategies, it is an honor and calling filled with rewards and growth given by the Lord Himself. It would be of my personal belief that such who fit this warning, step down from your altars and search out your own heart and your own salvation. Look within your own heart for the truth of your convictions and motives. Take the sin and your life to the Tabernacle of the Almighty and ask for forgiveness. If possible, restore that to those of whom you have taken.

The future of the children of this country depends on the simple truth of God's word to be taught. The truth of how to grow, and grow spiritually, is needed to develop into a right relationship with to God Himself. The apostle Paul has written, "Now I beseech you, brethren, mark them who cause division and offenses contrary to the doctrine which ye have learned; and avoid them for they that are such serve not the Lord Jesus Christ, but their own body, and by good words, and fair speeches deceive the hearts of the innocent." Romans 16: 17-18. We as a people must not turn to popular voices, though there are many out there that serve honestly and truthfully to God for good reasons.

However, we as individuals must run to Jesus. We must find Him on our own through prayer and Scripture. Our revival will only come from within ourselves. Finding our place in the Lord is to be level and honest with Him in the depths of our own hearts. To be level and honest within ourselves, knowing that nothing of our motives is hidden from Him. Over time, as we develop into His calling, may we hear our own hearts say: "In the Lord, I have seen love and know of its many yearning." In the Lord, I have seen peace and have known of its quietness and rest. In the Lord, I have seen joy and have known of its expectations. In the Lord, I have seen patience and have known of its strengths. In the Lord, I have seen hope and have known of its surety. In the Lord, I put my trust, for in Him is my security.

Chapter Eight

Final Thought and Prayer

In the things that I have written, I have exposed myself and a part of my life. I have revealed myself and have written of my relationship and my experience with the Almighty; take it as you will. I have shared my beginnings and growth in Him who I have described, and I have shared His word. I have recorded my experiences as they have occurred and in the sequence that they have happened. A sort of picture of a simple man's relationship with God above, where the man heard the thoughts and heart of God and obeyed, having revelation and exposure of what would be called sin and what would be apparent judgment.

The Lord looks deep, whether in individuals, a small group of people, or an entire nation; nothing is hidden. If my purpose is not pure, and the words that I have written are not true, if the words that I have spoken are not found acceptable, appropriate, and adequate by the

Lord, then my prayer is that the Lord take me home. However, if what I say is of the truth, found acceptable, appropriate, and adequate by Him, then my prayer is to let me continue to be a blessing and to speak, "thus sayeth the Lord."

My hope is that everyone who has read these words will examine themselves, looking seriously and deeply, not to be ashamed, but to seek forgiveness, knowing that forgiveness is given for finding the relationship He offers. I am humbled to think that the Lord has chosen me as He has and has revealed Himself as He saw fit. Who am I? I have earned and deserved nothing as I have received. Today I continue to function in life as I have always done, and as anyone would be expected to do. I know there is more for me, as I remain encouraged and expectant that whatever the Lord gives will be perfect. Day to day, I search for the Lord and, at times, crying out from my heart for Him, longing to know more of Him. This is my continual quest. I know down deep that there is more, maybe a word or a message, even the Lord expressing His love toward me. My spiritual life continues to grow, as I have seen it go from being a soldier clad in the armor of God knowing of serious issues, to being more at peace than ever. I do not consider myself equal, by any means, to those called of God for His purpose. Those who have had dreams and visions were matched with their faith that accomplished powerful service. I am merely a simple man who experienced what I have. Day to day I try to obey, looking daily in my heart to find His heart and His continual plan for me. I am waiting and I am patient.

Chapter 9

O Lord, I love you. I am with You in Your Tabernacle forever. Lift me up as You have done, I pray. I cry and open my heart to You. I am thankful that You know me, and I rejoice. I am at peace because You are there, and I feel Your presence in my heart. My heart is lifted and freed when You speak to me. My heart is at rest when I am in Your presence. I enter into Your rest, as I have strength and knowledge. I enter into Your rest, to refresh myself, being thankful that You are there to cover me and to keep me from the snare of evil and the grip of sin. You have washed me with Your blood, and cleansed me with Your presence. To You, my Lord, I yield. To you, my Lord, I trust. To You, my Lord, I give myself to the best of my strength, to the best of my hope, to the best as I know how. Your heart is what I seek. Your heart is what I cry for. To know You, to see You again, and to be with You, is the beginning of life for me. It is the beginning of understanding You that is the beginning of love. It is Your love that I must know. It is Your love that I must share. It is Your love that all must see. To You, my Lord, do I give my life. In You my Lord, does my heart long for, and in You, O Lord, is life. My weakness surrounds me, but Your strength lifts me. My suspicions confuse me, but Your word directs me. My sin convicts me, but Your blood frees me. My heart strays, but Your heart redirects. My mind fails, but your wisdom brings truth. I rejoice in that I have seen Your face. I am honored to have seen Your scars. I am broken to have seen Your eyes, and I am enlightened to have seen the light of Your eyes. I am blessed to have seen eternity within You. I am blessed to be taught. You teach me because You are my Father. I am Your son who must learn. I am a Jew who must obey, and a Jew who is free. I am a gentile who must observe, and I am a gentile forgiven. I am in You, You are in me, and together we live...

www.ingramcontent.com/pod-product-compliance
Lightning Source LLC
LaVergne TN
LVHW021735060526
838200LV00052B/3285